This Book Belongs To

_____

_____

_____

Letter Tracing
Alphabet Writing Practice

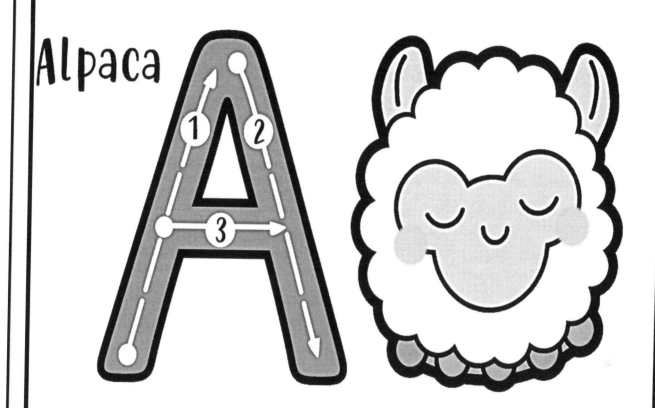

Alpaca

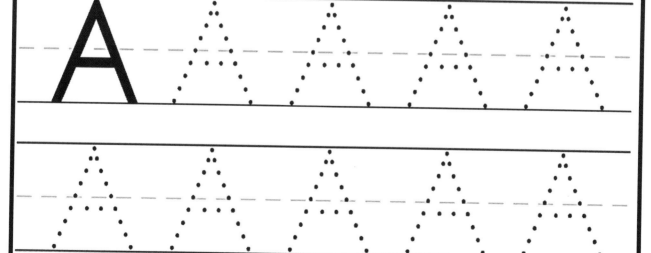

Trace & Color Letters

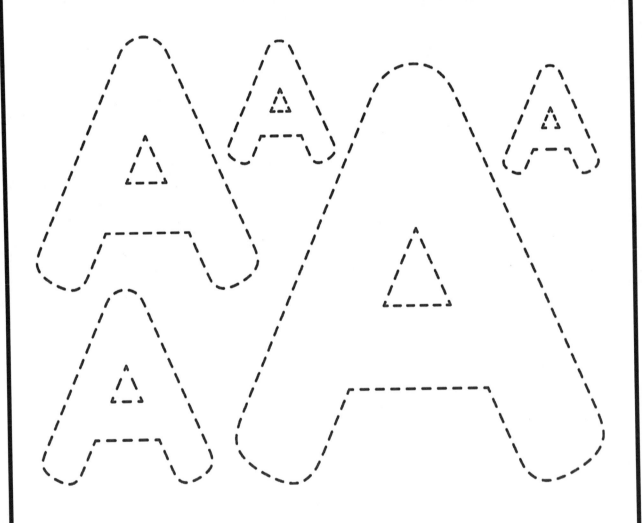

Letter Tracing
Alphabet Writing Practice

A is for Ant

Trace the letters with a pencil. Then practice writing the letters on the lines

Letter Tracing
Alphabet Writing Practice

Bear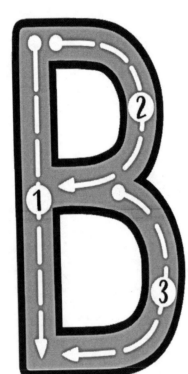

B B B B B

B B B B B

Trace & Color Letters

Letter Tracing
Alphabet Writing Practice

B is for Bear

Trace the letters with a pencil. Then practice writing the letters on the lines

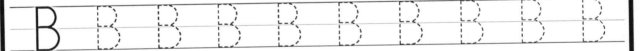

Letter Tracing
Alphabet Writing Practice

Cat

Trace & Color Letters

Letter Tracing
Alphabet Writing Practice

C is for Crab

Trace the letters with a pencil. Then practice writing the letters on the lines

Letter Tracing
Alphabet Writing Practice

Dog

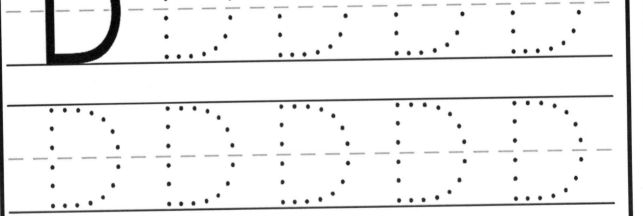

Trace & Color Letters

Letter Tracing
Alphabet Writing Practice

D is for Deer

Trace the letters with a pencil. Then practice writing the letters on the lines

Letter Tracing
Alphabet Writing Practice

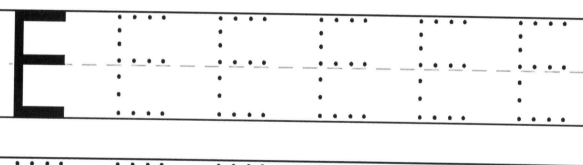

Trace & Color Letters

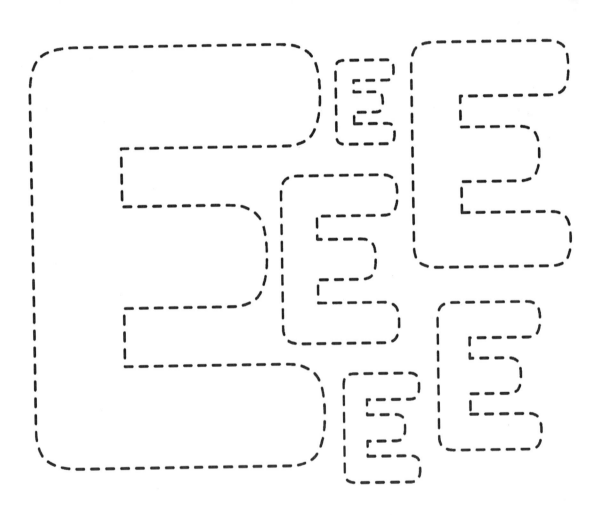

Letter Tracing
Alphabet Writing Practice

E is for Elephant

Trace the letters with a pencil. Then practice writing the letters on the lines

Letter Tracing
Alphabet Writing Practice

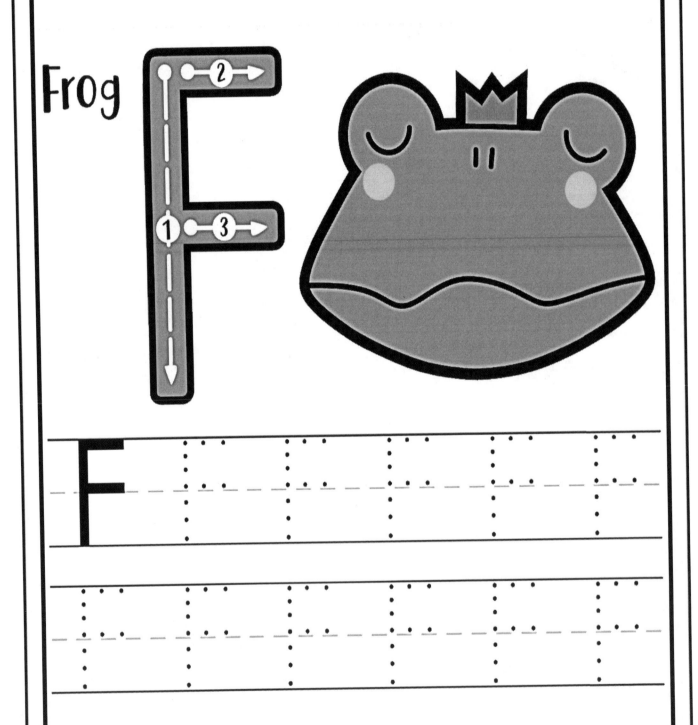

Trace & Color Letters

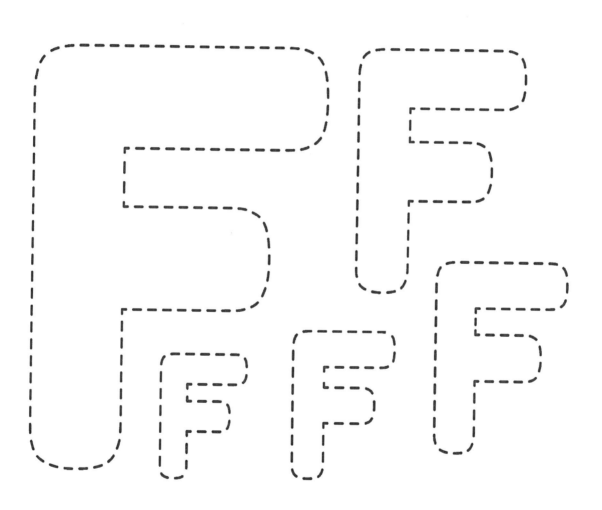

Letter Tracing
Alphabet Writing Practice

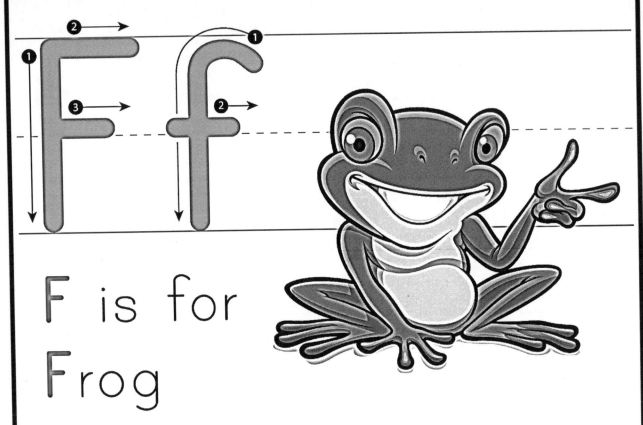

F is for Frog

Trace the letters with a pencil. Then practice writing the letters on the lines

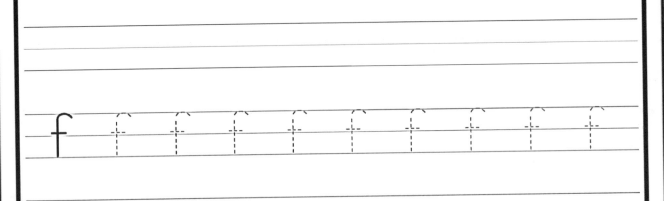

Letter Tracing
Alphabet Writing Practice

Giraffe

Trace & Color Letters

Letter Tracing
Alphabet Writing Practice

G is for Goldfish

Trace the letters with a pencil. Then practice writing the letters on the lines

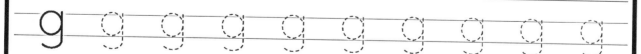

Letter Tracing
Alphabet Writing Practice

Horse

Trace & Color Letters

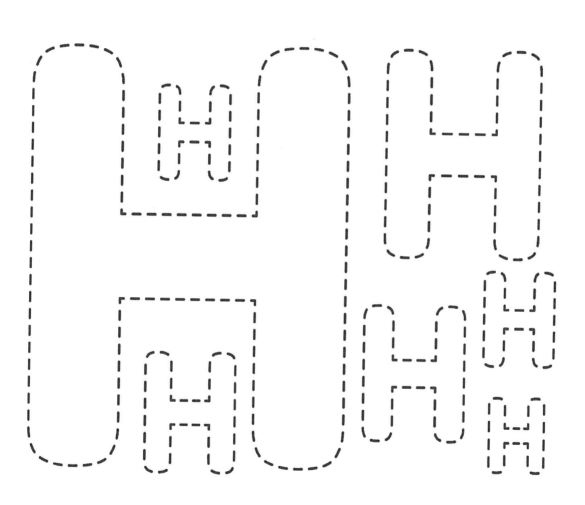

Letter Tracing
Alphabet Writing Practice

H is for Horse

Trace the letters with a pencil. Then practice writing the letters on the lines

Letter Tracing
Alphabet Writing Practice

Trace & Color Letters

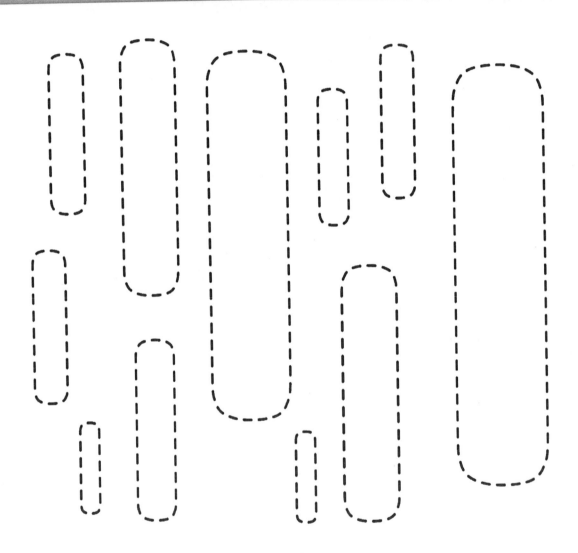

Letter Tracing
Alphabet Writing Practice

I is for Ibex

Trace the letters with a pencil. Then practice writing the letters on the lines

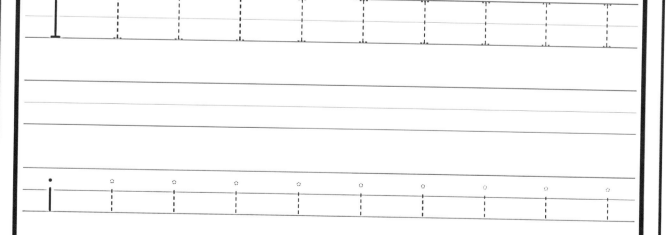

Letter Tracing
Alphabet Writing Practice

Jaguar

Trace & Color Letters

Letter Tracing
Alphabet Writing Practice

Koala

Trace & Color Letters

Letter Tracing
Alphabet Writing Practice

K is for Kangaroo

Trace the letters with a pencil. Then practice writing the letters on the lines

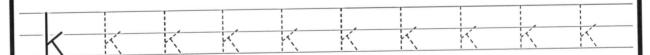

Letter Tracing
Alphabet Writing Practice

Lion

Trace & Color Letters

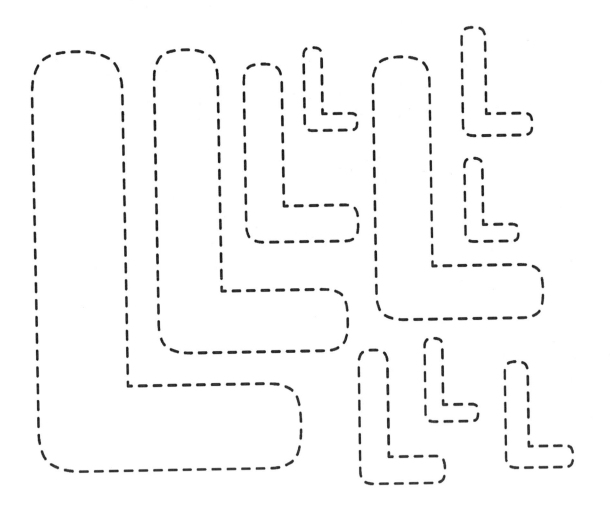

Letter Tracing
Alphabet Writing Practice

Name:

L is for Lion

Trace the letters with a pencil. Then practice writing the letters on the lines

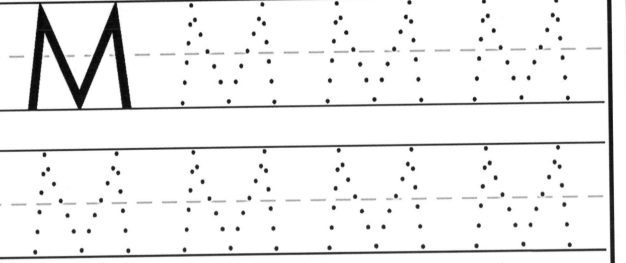

Trace & Color Letters

Letter Tracing
Alphabet Writing Practice

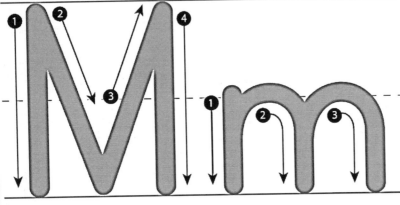

M is for Mouse

Trace the letters with a pencil. Then practice writing the letters on the lines

Letter Tracing
Alphabet Writing Practice

Narwahl

Trace & Color Letters

Letter Tracing
Alphabet Writing Practice

N is for Nautilus

Trace the letters with a pencil. Then practice writing the letters on the lines

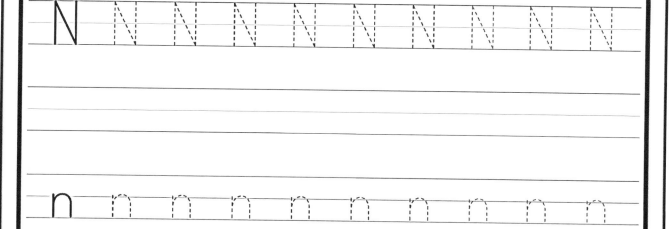

Letter Tracing
Alphabet Writing Practice

Owl

Trace & Color Letters

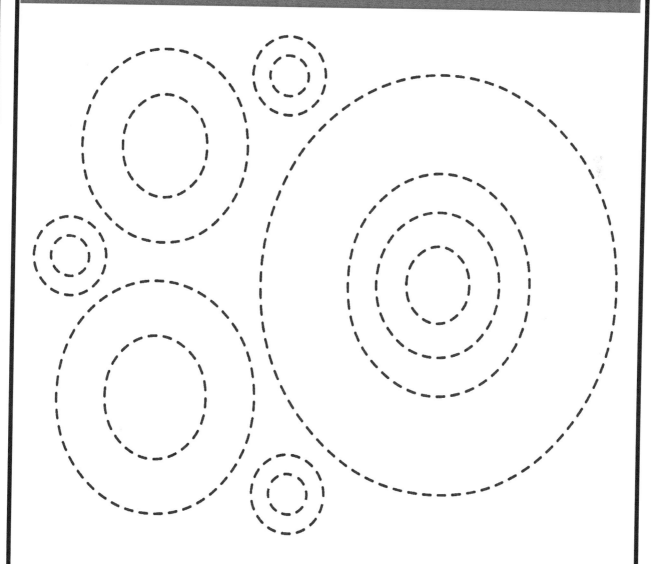

Letter Tracing
Alphabet Writing Practice

O is for Owl

Trace the letters with a pencil. Then practice writing the letters on the lines

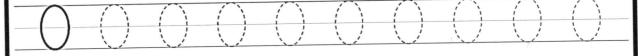

Letter Tracing
Alphabet Writing Practice

Penguin

Trace & Color Letters

Letter Tracing
Alphabet Writing Practice

P is for Panda

Trace the letters with a pencil. Then practice writing the letters on the lines

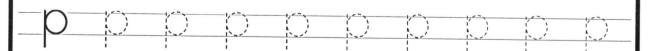

Letter Tracing
Alphabet Writing Practice

Quokka

Trace & Color Letters

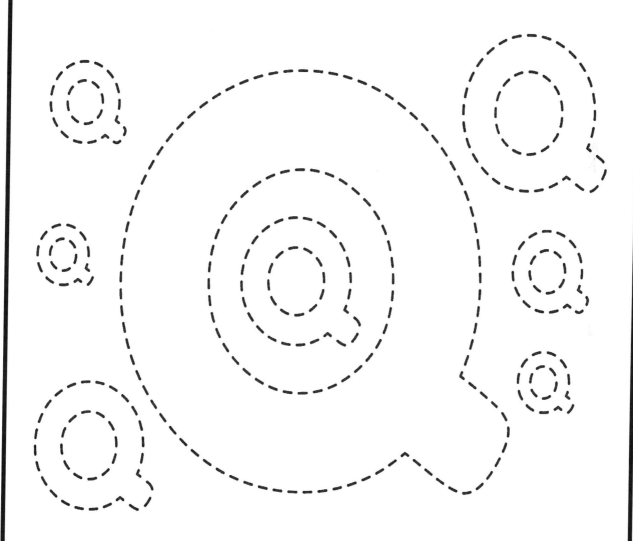

Letter Tracing
Alphabet Writing Practice

Q is for Quail

Trace the letters with a pencil. Then practice writing the letters on the lines

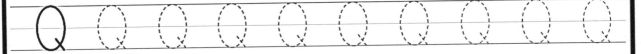

Letter Tracing
Alphabet Writing Practice

Rabbit

Trace & Color Letters

Letter Tracing
Alphabet Writing Practice

R is for Raccoon

Trace the letters with a pencil. Then practice writing the letters on the lines

R R R R R R R R R

r r r r r r r r r r

Letter Tracing
Alphabet Writing Practice

Squid

Trace & Color Letters

Letter Tracing
Alphabet Writing Practice

S is for Squirrel

Trace the letters with a pencil. Then practice writing the letters on the lines

Letter Tracing
Alphabet Writing Practice

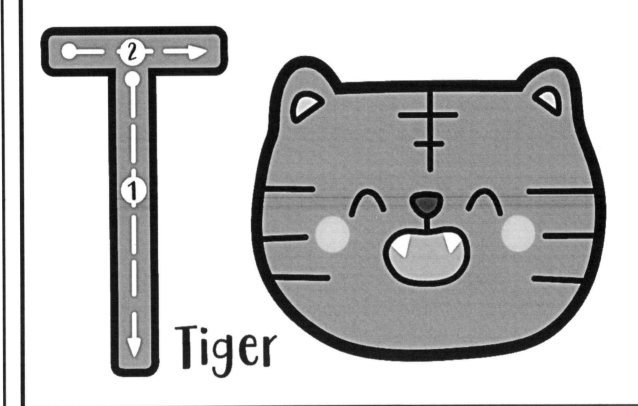

Tiger

Trace & Color Letters

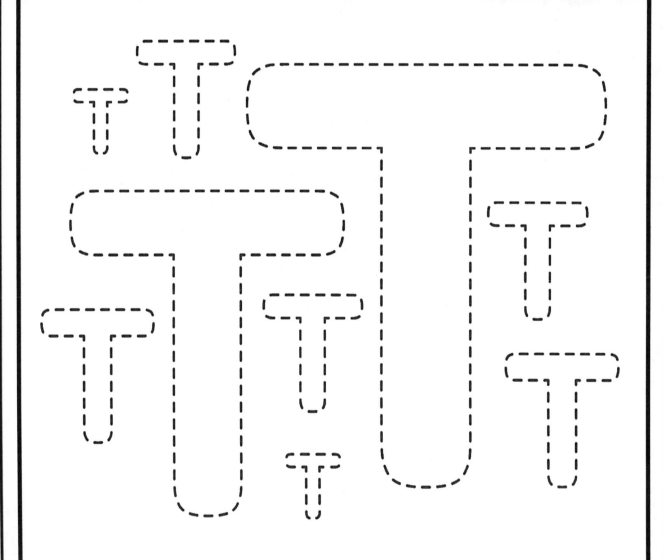

Letter Tracing
Alphabet Writing Practice

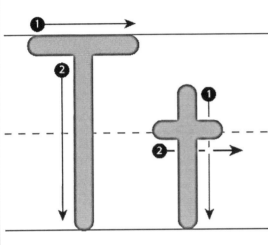

T is for Tiger

Trace the letters with a pencil. Then practice writing the letters on the lines

Letter Tracing
Alphabet Writing Practice

Trace & Color Letters

Letter Tracing
Alphabet Writing Practice

Name:

U is for
Umbrellabird

Trace the letters with a pencil. Then practice writing the letters on the lines

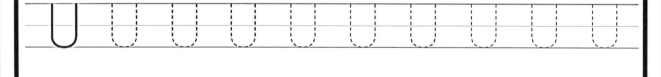

Letter Tracing
Alphabet Writing Practice

Vulture

Trace & Color Letters

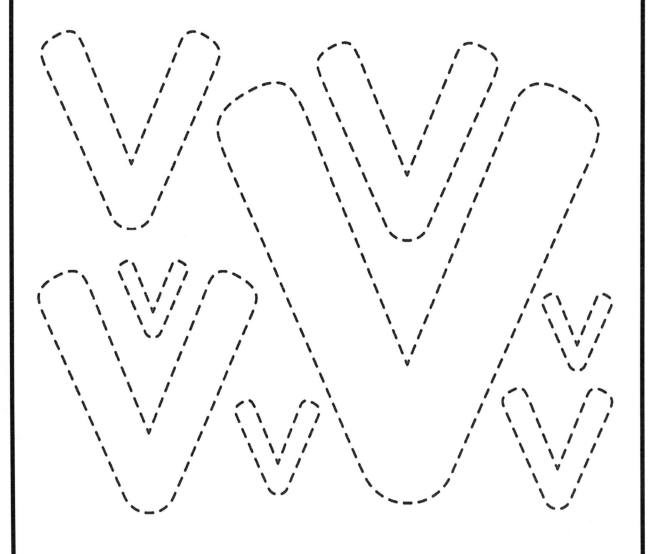

Letter Tracing
Alphabet Writing Practice

V is for Vulture

Trace the letters with a pencil. Then practice writing the letters on the lines

V

v

Letter Tracing
Alphabet Writing Practice

Walrus

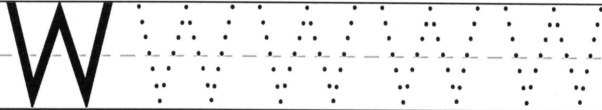

Trace & Color Letters

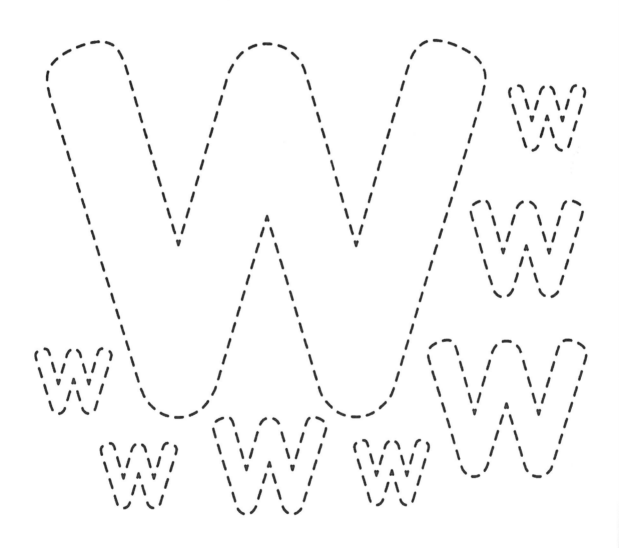

Letter Tracing
Alphabet Writing Practice

W is for Wolf

Trace the letters with a pencil. Then practice writing the letters on the lines

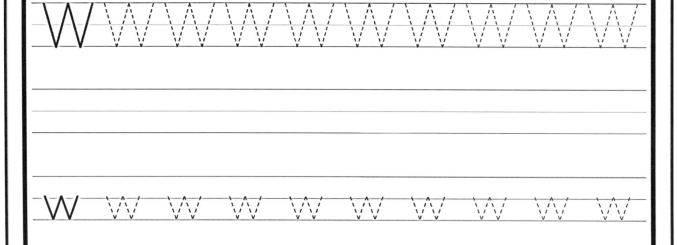

Letter Tracing
Alphabet Writing Practice

Xantus

Trace & Color Letters

Letter Tracing
Alphabet Writing Practice

X is for X-ray Fish

Trace the letters with a pencil. Then practice writing the letters on the lines

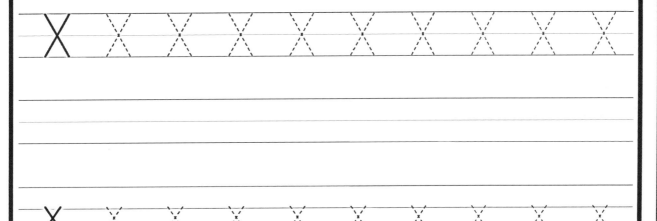

Letter Tracing
Alphabet Writing Practice

yak

Trace & Color Letters

Letter Tracing
Alphabet Writing Practice

Y is for
Yak

Trace the letters with a pencil. Then practice writing the letters on the lines

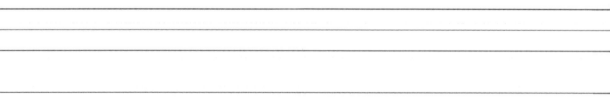

Letter Tracing
Alphabet Writing Practice

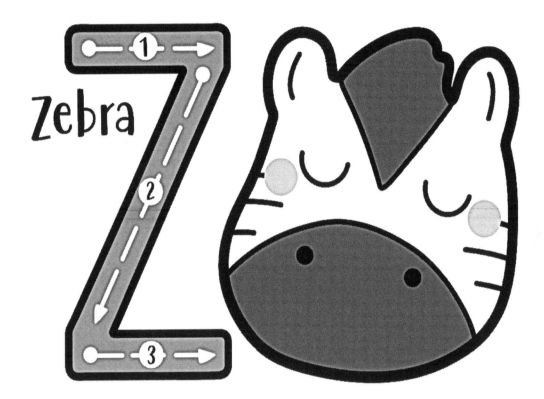

Trace & Color Letters

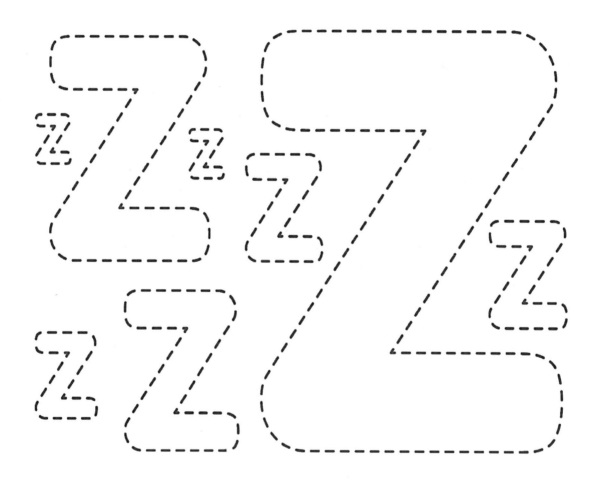

Letter Tracing
Alphabet Writing Practice

Z is for Zebra

Trace the letters with a pencil. Then practice writing the letters on the lines

Email us at
SurprisesPdf@gmail.com
to get free extras

just titre the email - **Workbook For Kids** -
And we will send some extra
surprises your way !

Trace the letters

A A A A A A A

B B B B B B B

C C C C C C C

D D D D D D D

E E E E E E E

F F F F F F F

Trace the letters

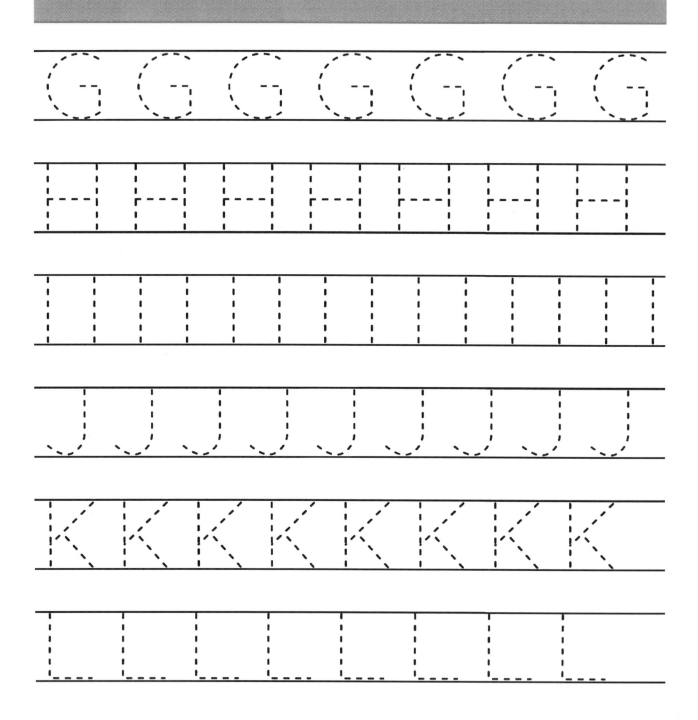

Trace the letters

Bonus Activity

Outstanding work!

**You're so good at what you do.
I'm so proud of your effort**

| SQUARE | CIRCLE | TRIANGLE | RECTANGER |

Bonus Activity

Trace The Shapes

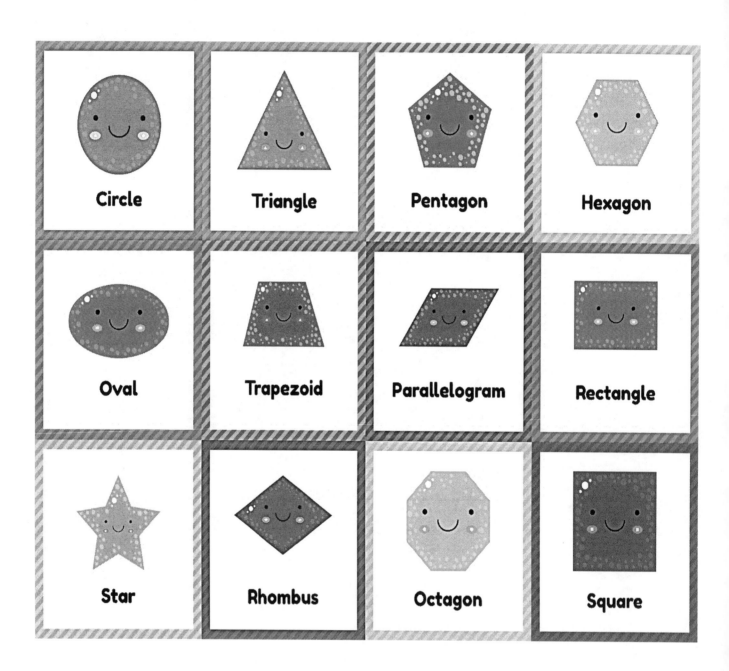

Trace the shapes

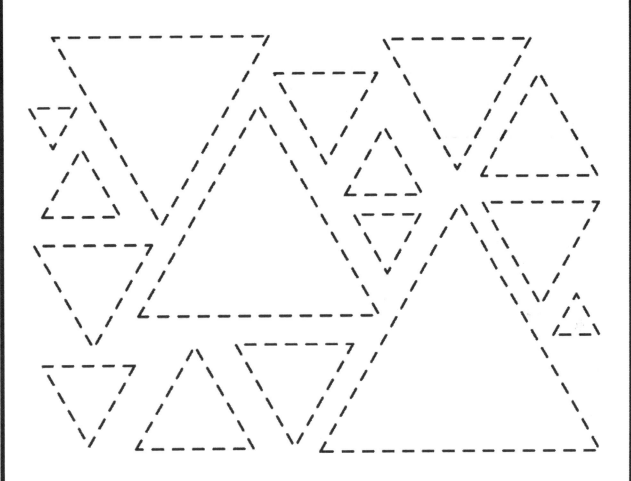

Trace the shapes

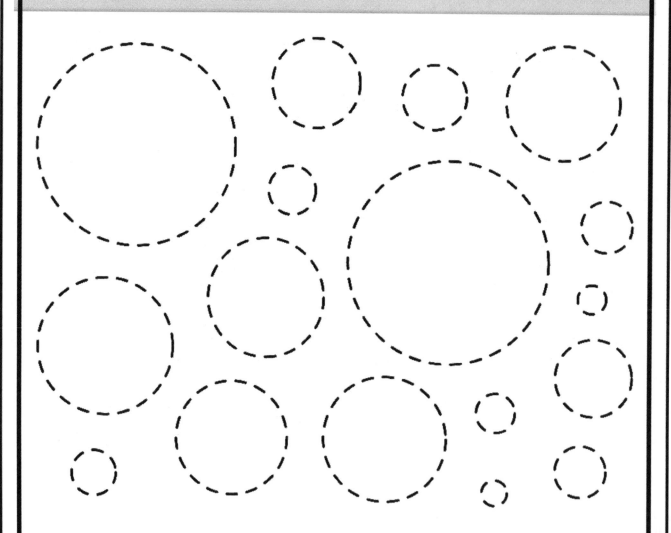

Trace the shapes

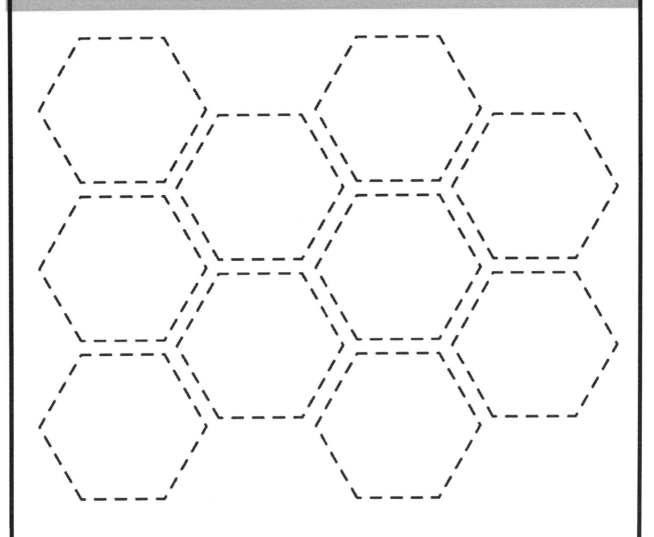

Trace the shapes

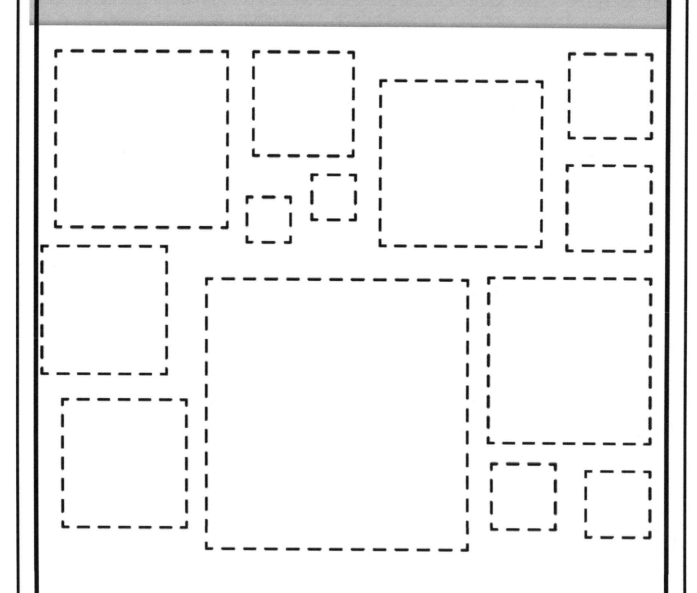

Trace the shapes

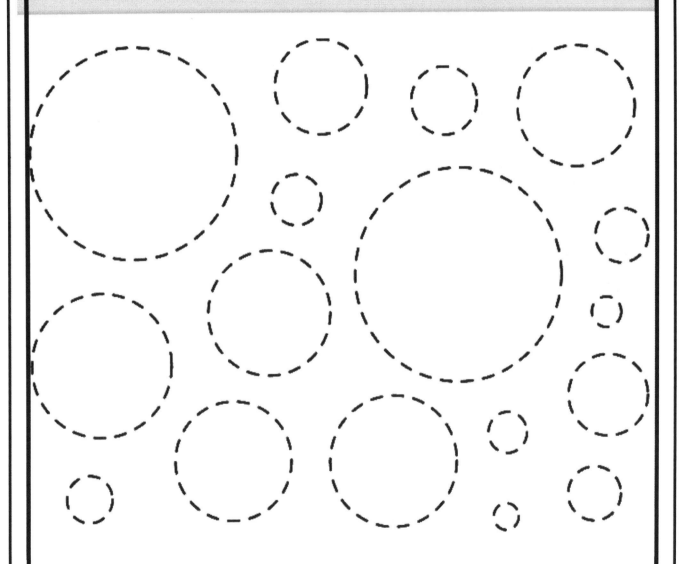

Trace the shapes

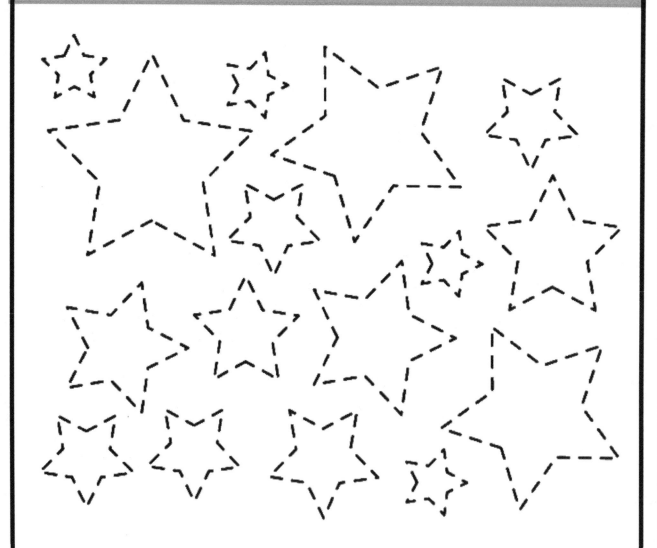

Trace the shapes

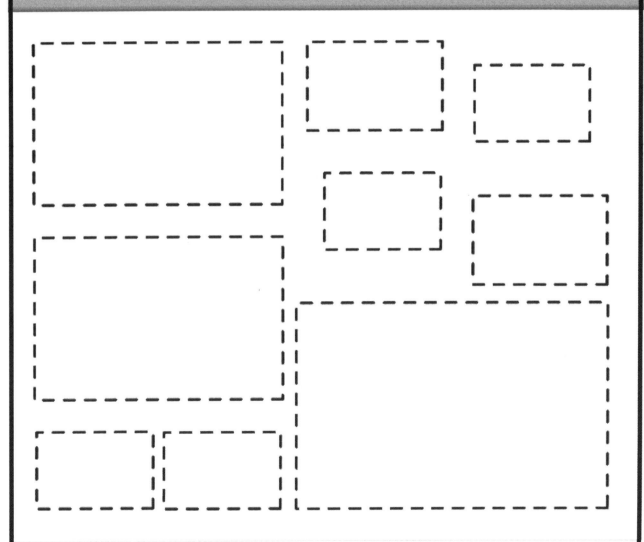

Trace the shapes

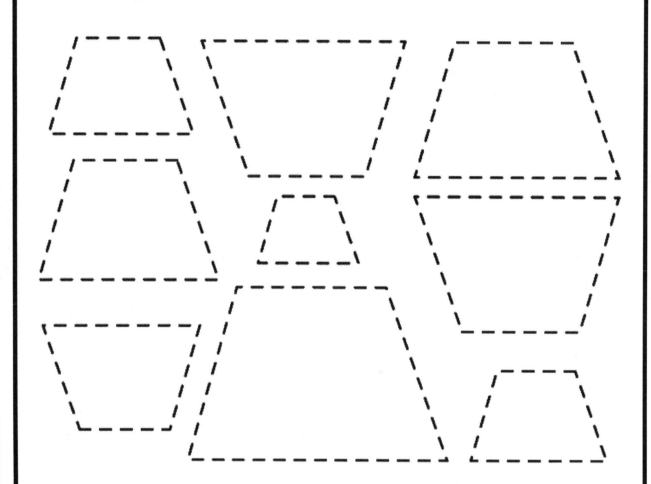

Trace the shapes

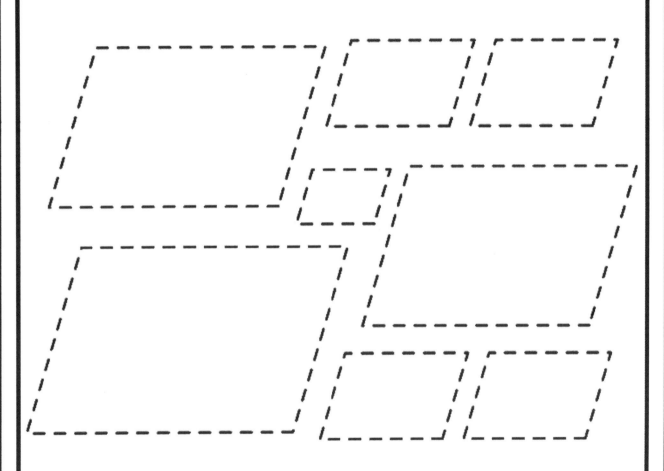

Trace the shapes

Trace the shapes

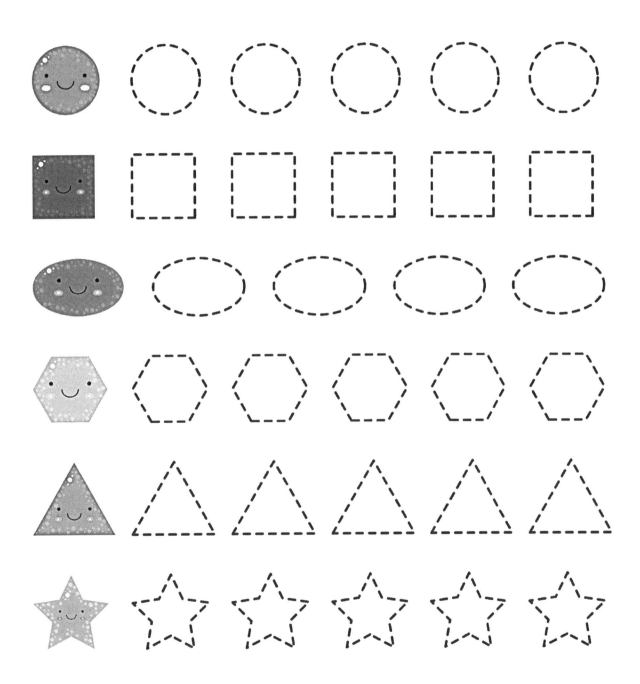

Wow, you are so skilled!

Your effort makes me proud

PART TWO

NUMBERS TRACING

One apple

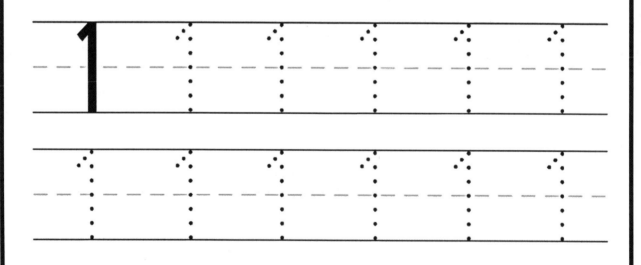

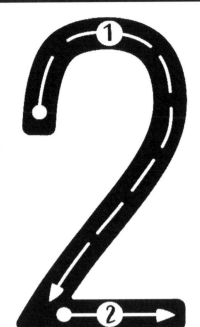

Two pineapples

2 2 2 2 2

2 2 2 2 2

two two two

two two two

Three strawberries

3

Four lemons

4 4 4 4 4

4 4 4 4 4

four four four

four four four

Five oranges

5 5 5 5 5
5 5 5 5 5

five five five
five five five

Six broccolis

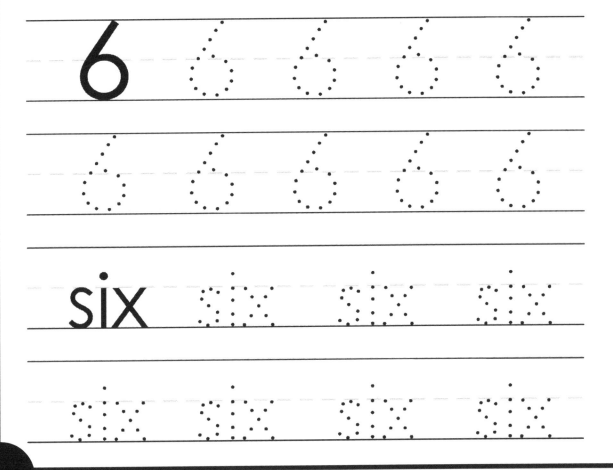

Seven tomatos

7 7 7 7 7 7

7 7 7 7 7 7

seven seven

seven seven

Eight eggplants

8

eight

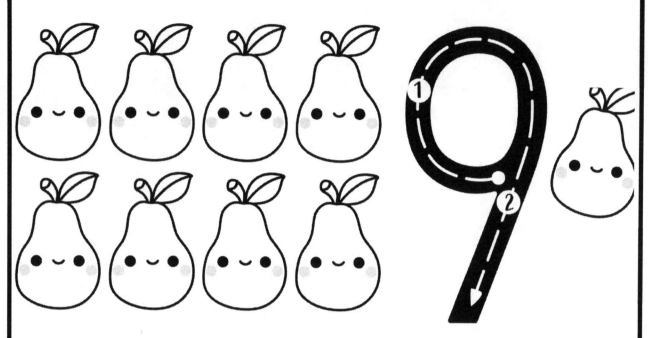

Nine pears

9 9 9 9 9

9 9 9 9 9

nine nine nine

nine nine nine

Ten carrtos

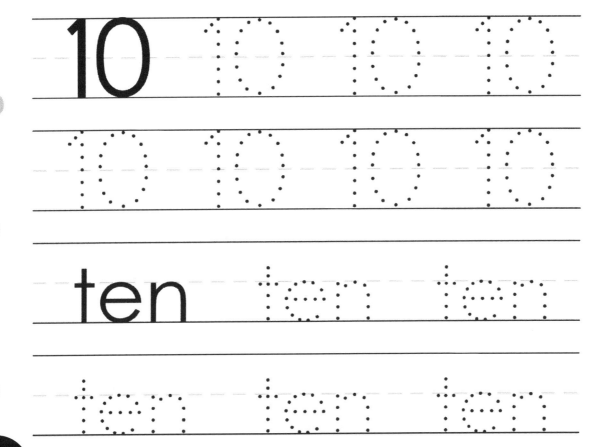

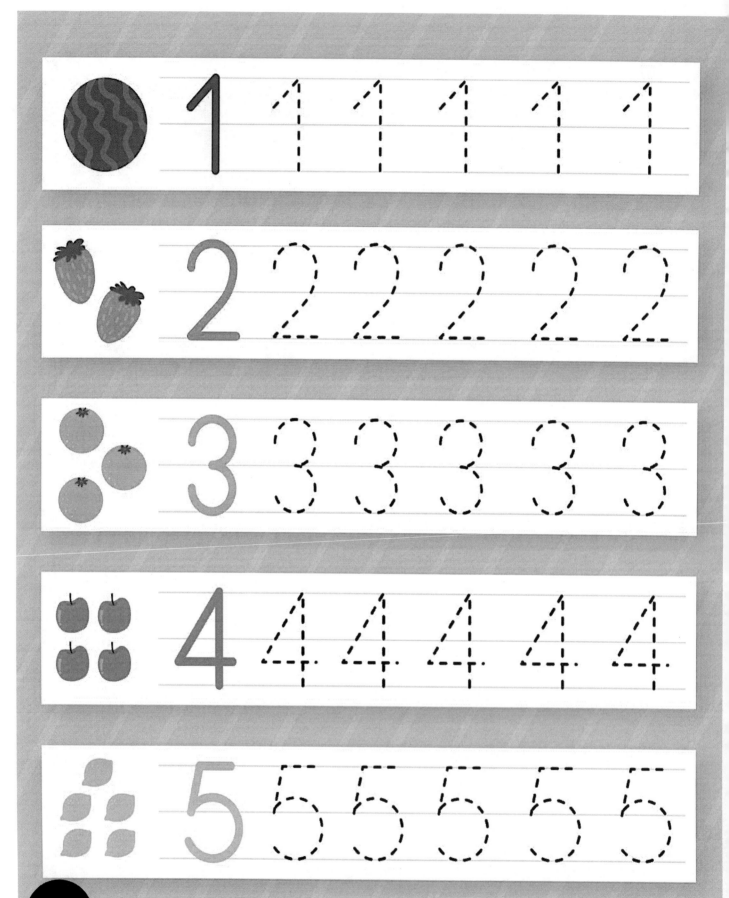

6 6 6 6 6 6
7 7 7 7 7 7
8 8 8 8 8 8
9 9 9 9 9 9
10 10 10 10 10 10

Made in the USA
Columbia, SC
21 June 2025